Instruments and Music

Voices

Daniel Nunn

Heinemann Library
Chicago, Illinois

www.capstonepub.com
Visit our website to find out more information about Heinemann-Raintree books.

To order:

☎ Phone 800-747-4992

💻 Visit www.capstonepub.com to browse our catalog and order online.

© 2012 Heinemann Library
an imprint of Capstone Global Library, LLC
Chicago, Illinois

Edited by Dan Nunn, Rebecca Rissman, and Sian Smith
Designed by Joanna Hinton-Malivoire
Picture research by Mica Brancic
Production by Victoria Fitzgerald
Originated by Capstone Global Library Ltd
Printed in the United States of America in Eau Claire, Wisconsin.
072013   007594RP

15 14 13 12 11
10 9 8 7 6 5 4 3 2 1

Library of Congress Cataloging-in-Publication Data
Nunn, Daniel.
  Voices / Daniel Nunn.
    p. cm.—(Instruments and music)
  Includes bibliographical references and index.
  ISBN 978-1-4329-5061-3 (hc)—ISBN 978-1-4329-5068-2 (pb)
1. Singing—Juvenile literature. I. Title.
  ML1400.N86 2012
  783—dc22   2010044782

Acknowledgments
We would like to thank the following for permission to reproduce photographs: Getty Images pp. 7 (Redferns/Odile Noel), 12 (Hans-Martin Issler), 18 (for the Tribeca Film Festival/Roger Kisby); Photolibrary pp. 4 (Corbis), 8 (Janine Wiedel), 9 (LOOK-foto/Ulla Lohmann), 10 (Radius Images), 14 (Ingram Publishing RF), 15 (White/John Molloy), 17 (Westend61/Hans Huber), 21 (Radius Images), 22 (All Canada Photos/Glenn Bartley), 23 top (Ingram Publishing RF), 23 middle top (Moodboard Moodboard), 23 middle bottom (Glow Images, Inc.), 23 bottom (White/John Molloy); Shutterstock pp. 5 (© Jason Stitt), 6 (© Dmitriy Shironosov), 11 (© Jack.Qi), 13 (© Dmitriy Shironosov), 16 (© withGod), 19 (© Andreas Gradin), 20 (© Anton Gvozdikov).

Cover photograph of villagers performing a traditional song and dance in Malawi, reproduced with permission of Getty Images (The Image Bank/Simon Rawles). Back cover photograph of a gospel choir reproduced with permission of Photolibrary (Radius Images).

We would like to thank Jenny Johnson, Nancy Harris, Dee Reid, and Diana Bentley for their assistance in the preparation of this book.

Every effort has been made to contact copyright holders of material reproduced in this book. Any omissions will be rectified in subsequent printings if notice is given to the publisher.

Contents

Musical Instruments

saxophone

guitar

People play many instruments to make music.

Some people use their voices to make music. This is called singing.

Singing

Some people sing along with other musical instruments.

Some people sing without any musical instruments.

Some people sing inside.

Some people sing outside.

Some people sing with other people.

Some people sing alone.

Opera singers can sing very loudly.

microphone

Pop singers use microphones to sound louder.

Humming and Whistling

Not all singing has words. You can hum a tune with your mouth closed.

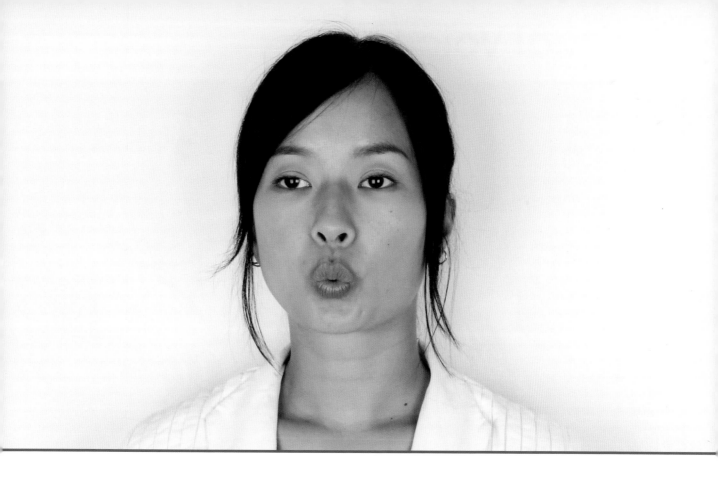

You can whistle a tune by blowing through your teeth and lips.

Unusual Voices

Throat singers sing using their throats.

Yodelers sing low notes and high notes all in one breath.

Beatboxers use their voices to make the sounds of drums.

Rappers speak songs instead of singing them.

Why Do People Sing?

Some people sing for work.

Some people sing just for fun!

Birdsong

People are not the only animals that sing. Some birds can sing many different songs!

Picture Glossary

 **hum** sing or make music with your lips closed

 **microphone** something you sing into to make your voice louder

 **note** sound made by your voice or another musical instrument

 **whistle** make a musical sound by blowing through your teeth or lips

Index

Notes for Parents and Teachers

Before reading

Explain that people use their voices for talking, but they also use them for singing. Discuss different types of singing with the children. What different types of singing can they think of? What types of singing do they enjoy?

After reading

Discuss the fact that singing doesn't only mean singing words. Encourage the children to try to make different sounds with their voices. Ask them to try singing in a high voice, a low voice, a quiet voice, a loud voice, and so on. Can they recognize when people are singing in a high voice or a low voice?

Extra information

People have vocal folds, which are used for talking, singing, laughing, crying, and so on. There are three parts: the lungs, which produce air and make the air vibrate through the vocal folds (like a woodwind instrument); the larynx, which changes the length of the folds to make the sound higher or lower (like a brass instrument); and the mouth, which changes the sound to make it louder or quieter. Men have lower voices than women and children because their vocal folders are larger. Whistling is different to singing because it does not use the voice. It works in the same sort of way as a wind instrument. Air is blown through a hole made by the lips.